FOR DUPLICATES ADDRESS.......

Altman & Edelman,
.....Battle Creek, Mich.

me

mother
1914

NEVER A PAL LIKE MOTHER

VINTAGE SONGS
& PHOTOGRAPHS
OF THE ONE WHO'S
ALWAYS TRUE

DUST-TO-DIGITAL
ATLANTA, GA

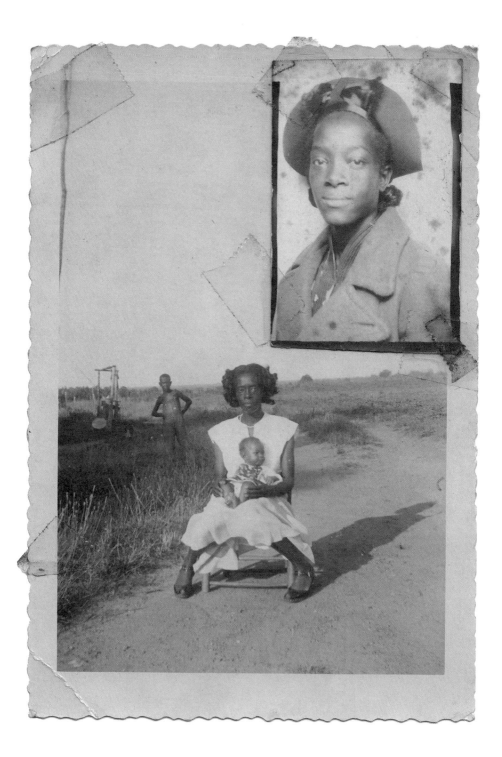

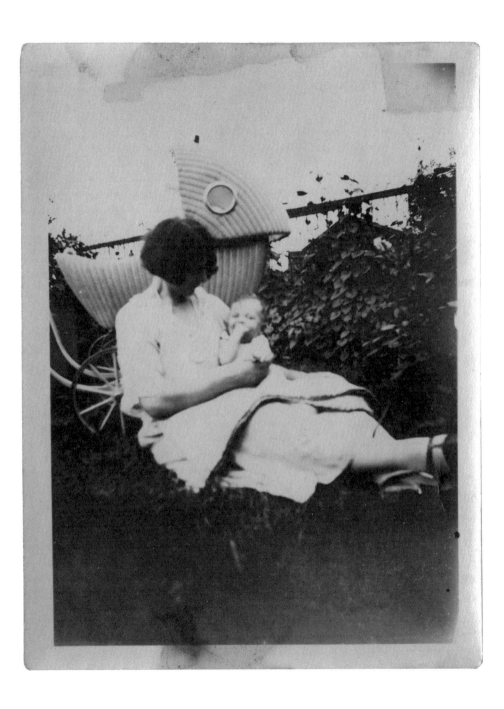

-1941

FOREWORD

From our vantage point in the twenty-first century, it is hard to imagine an entire collection of music as full of frank admiration and celebration, or mourning and native longing, as these songs about Mother. In popular music today, romantic love and all its attendant frustrations dominate the airwaves, but there was a time, in the early part of the twentieth century, when there were hundreds of recordings devoted to the most revered figure in every family. She was mostly idealized to the point of sainthood, without self-consciousness or irony. Much of the idealization came in part because of the hardships of the time, particularly in the poor South and Appalachia, where many of these songs originated. One was often permanently separated from one's mother in early adulthood, or late adolescence, either by distance or death. A longing suffused the rest of life: for home, the nurturing received (whether fantasized or real), and all those comforts that were singly personified by Mother. Out of that longing came these songs.

The songs in this collection wail, grieve, rock, celebrate, and worship Mother, and occasionally acknowledge her failings. As a whole, this music paints a rich and compelling portrait of a time that no longer exists.

We can feel our American past here: how we lived, how hard we worked, how we were a nation of travelers and wanderers, how we held fast to our faith, how great our losses were, how quickly death came, and how often our mothers were the rock and the lighthouse, the home inside our hearts. These songs could never be written in the age of jet travel, therapy, delayed adolescence, the internet, nor could they survive current popular ideas of human psychology. They are pristine and deeply wrought sonic images, unfiltered through modern expectations, and are all the more refreshing and thrilling for being so. Those of us who treasure American roots music are listening to the very center of its essence in this anthology: a nearly century-old collection of songs about the most important person in the entire lexicon.

—Rosanne Cash

BLESS HER HEART

Pappy O'Daniel—the biscuit baron, radio racon- teur, and eventual Governor of and Senator from Texas—had a fondness for reciting topical poetry during the radio broadcasts in which he and the Light Crust Dough Boys promoted Hillbilly Flour. One day in May, Flannery O'Connor happened to tune in to the broadcast, and happily, was listening as O'Daniel recited a special poem for Mother's Day. Later, in 1953, when her health had begun its long decline and she was living with her mother in Milledgeville, Georgia, O'Connor would remember O'Daniel's verses, and share them in a letter to Robert and Elizabeth Lowell. The poem, she wrote, went like this:

> *I had a mother. I had to have.*
> *I lover whether she's good or bad.*
> *I lover whether she's live or dead.*
> *Whether she's an angel or a old dopehead.*

"You poets express yourselves so well in so little space," she added.

There was a tinge of heresy in Pappy O'Daniel's reverie. Most Southern men of the era would be likely to describe their mothers as angels; however, to suggest that an alternative to "angel" could be anything other than "saint" was truly peculiar. (But O'Daniel was an Ohioan by birth, so his perspective may have been broader.) Still, his declaration of filial devotion was very much in tune with the popular culture of the day. The teenage rage of the 1950s and '60s had yet to sweep the land, and rather than being seen as, first, a square, and later a stooge of an oppressive ancien régime, Mother was still a figure to whom was due affectionate nostalgia— part and parcel of a longing for hearth and home.

OUT IN THE COLD WORLD, LONG WAYS FROM HOME

By the first half of the twentieth century, the era when the music in this compilation was recorded, separation from loved ones had become an accepted fact of life for several generations of Americans. Westward migration had cleft many families along generational lines, as young people left their elders in the East, rarely if ever to see them again. Dying on the battlefields of the Civil War, hundreds of thousands of boys and men knew there would be a vacant chair at their mother's table. Immigrants from Ireland and Germany and Italy said goodbye to their mothers as they prepared to cross the ocean to America, while African Americans in the South did the same as they boarded northbound trains. Another wave of young soldiers left home, headed for the hills of Cuba and the Philippine boondocks. Their sons

would write home from the trenches of Europe. Each generation knew what it was to miss home and mother.

This shared nostalgia became a mainstay of pop culture. In early country music, the mother song was a staple, from the genuinely heartbreaking to the maudlin. Throughout hillbilly music, Mama prays for her wayward son; she leaves a lamp shining for him in the window; she writes him letters. Her letter turns up in the breast pocket of the dying soldier, or cowboy, or railroad man; and after the son breathes his last, the letter, if a bullet hole has not rendered it illegible, is read by the fallen man's comrades, who then pine for their own faraway mothers. Some day, though, they'll shake their mothers' hands again—in that land beyond the blue, where no sad tears are shed and parting is no more.

Blues and black gospel singers missed their mamas too. Jaybird Coleman fantasized about going to heaven, not so much to "sit down by King Jesus"—though that too—but primarily to find his mother and "tell her how you treat me." Years later the Pilgrim Travelers sang in "I've Got a New Home" about the pleasures of reaching heaven, which include talking with Jesus. But Mother makes a cameo appearance in time for the finale, in which she and the son she's been praying for sit down and "talk things over." The ostensible gospel song concludes, "I love my mother because she's mine/She's mine/Yes, she's mine."

In the music of the era, Mother is not always dead or far away or both; just usually. If she's still on-hand, she has words of wisdom to impart, or admonitions: don't rub mustard in Grandpa's hat; no hillbilly-playing 'round here. Elvie Thomas' 1930 "Motherless Child Blues" *(Disc 2, Track 10)* is remarkable for many reasons, but perhaps the most startling is the suggestion that Mother might have a checkered past. "My mother told me just before she died/ . . . Said 'Daughter, daughter, please don't be like me/Don't fall in love with every man you see.'" Rev. Gates' 1929 sermon in this collection *(Disc 1, Track 9)* is similarly jaded. You ought to remain close to your mother, he advises, because she's the only one who can tell you who your real father is. Surely an angel, but perhaps not always a saint.

THE PICTURE ON THE WALL

For the Georgia Yellow Hammers *(Disc 2, Track 7)*, the full force of affection for the absent mother is bestowed on "an old and faded picture on the wall." Interior design specs might not make for the most mellifluous of choruses, but the story rings true. How many of the anonymous vintage photographs to be found in today's flea markets and antique shops once served their previous owners as mementos of faraway or long-dead loved ones?

Americans' increasing mobility coincided with the development and democratization of photography. Only the well-heeled among the early Western migrants

would have had painted miniatures of their mothers to
accompany them. By the Civil War, access to portraiture was still a somewhat elite privilege, but we know
that ambrotypes, cartes-de-visite, and tintypes of loved
ones were among many soldiers' personal effects. In
the years to come, commercial photo studios would
proliferate. In the very first weeks of the new century
came the Brownie camera, and it became increasingly
common for families of limited to middling resources

to own their own cameras. Though formal, professional portraiture would survive, the snapshot allowed for the creation of a whole new world of vernacular expression. Even the poorest people would be likely at some point in their lives to have access to photo booths.

Almost anyone could have a photograph of his or her mother, whether in the wallet or on the wall.

Audiophiles who love the recorded music of the early twentieth century are attracted in part by the intimacy that old records impart. Because of the comparative simplicity of the technology, experiencing music through the medium of a 78 rpm record is closely akin to staring into an old photograph, seeing a moment of the long-ago past with a clarity that's only one step removed from the real thing. Today's methods of capturing and reproducing sound and light produce an experience that may be clearer, but is not as close. The music and photography offered in *Never A Pal Like Mother* come from a span of years when the innovations of modern life began not only to draw us apart, but to bring us closer together.

The gift of recorded sound and photography is that they compensate for absence. Sometimes nostalgia is the mother of invention.

—*Sarah Bryan*

SHE WAS THE FIRST TO EVER LOVE ME

AND
SHE'LL BE
THE LAST ONE
I FORGET

Louvin Brothers
God Bless Her, She's My Mother

ME – MOTHER   1932

Who sang to you rock a bye my baby
Who held you close to her breast
Who told you the story of the Sandman
and loved you gently to rest
Who made your childhood happy
and shared every sorrow with you
No one else but mother
The pal that is always true

Doc Hopkins
The Pal That's Always True

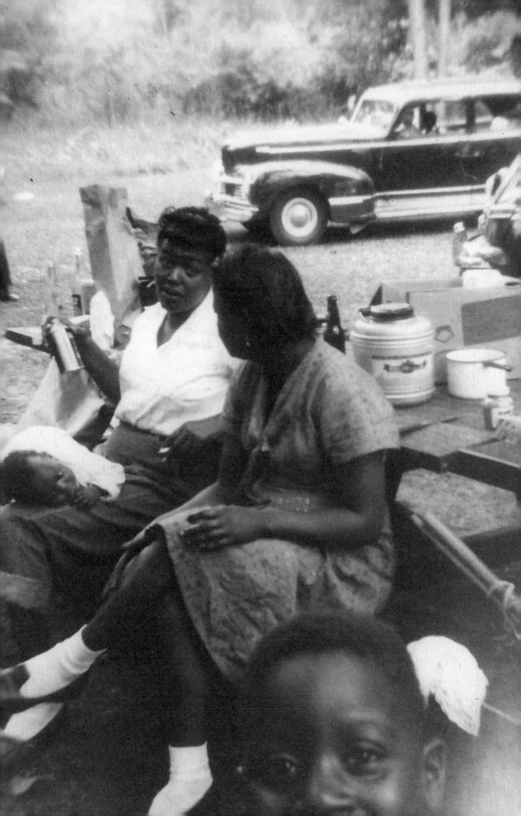

HIS MOTHER
SO GOOD
DID ALL THAT
SHE COULD
TO RAISE HIM
AND TEACH HIM
WITH CARE

Mr. and Mrs. Harmon E. Helmick
Little Moses

Don't give her any
back chat or insolence
For you will be punished
by the omnipotent
A mother's love
is a bless on creation
You could never find
a greater and stronger affection

Mighty Destroyer
Mother's Love

NO MORE
DANCING MAMA
NO MORE
PLAYING CARDS
FROM THIS DAY ON
I WILL SERVE MY GOD

Washington Phillips
A Mother's Last Word to Her Daughter

JAN • 57

APR • 57

SO MANY
WAYS YOU CAN
BREAK YOUR
MOTHER'S
HEART

....

Rev. J.M. Gates

You Mother Heart Breakers

Mother called her child
to her dying bed
She softly whispered
these are the words she said
Child I'm going away,
meet me at the coming day
I'm gonna leave you
in the hands of my God
Mother told her child,
Child I'm going to die
I'm gonna leave you
in the hands of my God

Lil McClintock
Mother Called Her Child to Her Dying Bed

I'M SMILING

AS I GO ON

TO MEET MOTHER

SHE'S WAITING

FOR ME

BY THE BRIGHT

CRYSTAL SEA

Cecil Surratt & His West Virginia Ramblers
The Bright Crystal Sea

Yes I know
that she will know me
In those mansions bright and fair
Mother's love can n'er forget me
And I'm sure she'll
know me there

L.V. Jones and His Virginia Singing Class
Will My Mother Know Me There?

DISC 1

-1- LOUVIN BROTHERS
God Bless Her, She's My Mother 29 April 1956

-2- DOC HOPKINS
The Pal That's Always True 9 October 1936

-3- MR. AND MRS. HARMON E. HELMICK
Little Moses 29 May 1931

-4- WILLIAM MCCOY
Mama Blues 6 December 1927

-5- EARL MCDONALD'S ORIGINAL
LOUISVILLE JUG BAND
Mama's Little Sunny Boy 30 March 1927

-6- MIGHTY DESTROYER
Mother's Love 8 April 1941

-7- FRANKIE "HALF-PINT" JAXON
Mama Don't Allow It 29 July 1933

-8- MADDOX BROTHERS & ROSE
Mama Says It's Naughty 1947

-9- REV. J.M. GATES
You Mother Heart Breakers 18 March 1929

-10- WADE MAINER
**Mother Came to Get Her
Boy from Jail** 15 February 1936

DISC 2

-1- J.P. RYAN
Mother's Gone 18 February 1930

-2- GOLDEN GATE JUBILEE QUARTET
Stand in the Test in Judgment 3:05 4 August 1937

-3- LEO SOILEAU
Mama, Where You At? 19 October 1928

-4- JAN WYSOWSKI
Kujawiak Babki (Grandmother's Dance) 8 May 1929

-5- BOB WILLS
Tie Me to Your Apron Strings Again 8 June 1937

-6- SHORTBUCKLE ROARK & FAMILY
My Mother's Hands 4 November 1928

-7- GEORGIA YELLOW HAMMERS
The Picture on the Wall 9 August 1927

-8- CAROLINA TWINS
Where Is My Mamma? 2 November 1928

-9- MILTON BROWN & HIS MUSICAL BROWNIES
I've Got the Blues for Mammy 3 March 1936

-10- ELVIE THOMAS
Motherless Child Blues ca. March 1930

NEVER A PAL LIKE MOTHER

PRODUCED BY
Steven Lance Ledbetter

FOREWORD BY
Rosanne Cash

ESSAY BY
Sarah Bryan

ORIGINAL PHOTOGRAPHS
Sarah Bryan, Betty Curl, Dust-to-Digital
Archives, Magda Freeman, Sarah Ledbetter,
Jim Linderman, Rob Millis and David Murray

ART DIRECTION AND DESIGN
Debbie Berne Design

PRODUCTION ASSISTANCE
April G. Ledbetter, Rob Millis and Hilary Staff

ORIGINAL 78S
Joe Bussard, Peter Honig, Frank Mare, Roger Misiewicz,
Dick Spottswood and Jonathan Ward

RECORD TRANSFERS
David Anderson, Chris King, Jack Towers,
Jonathan Ward and John Wilby

AUDIO RESTORATION AND MASTERING
Michael Graves, Osiris Studio

ISBN 978-0-9817342-3-1

DUST-TO-DIGITAL
PO BOX 54743
ATLANTA, GA 30308
INFO@DUST-DIGITAL.COM

PRINTED IN CHINA

IDA   IVA   EVA

The Famous HANNA Triplet's

WENDT, PHOTO ARTIST   Boonton, N. J.